The Grief

WITH YOU IN M...
FLAMING FLOWERS

A SURVIVORS MANUAL FOR DEATH BY OVERDOSE

Marie Minnich

1st Edition

Copyright February 2016 by Marie Minnich

ISBN: 978-1530455430

The Grief Chronicles: With You in My Eyes Like Flaming Flowers

All rights reserved. No part of this book may be reproduced or transmitted in any form or by any means, electronic or mechanical, including photocopying, recording, or by any information storage and retrieval system, without permission in writing from the copyright owner, other than excerpts for purposes of review.

Also available from the author:
My Daughters Addiction: A Thief in the Family: Hardwired for Heroin
Cover photography: Marie Minnich

DISCLAIMER: This book details the author's personal experiences with grief recovery after a substance passing. The author is not licensed as a certified grief counselor, consultant, teacher, psychologist, or psychiatrist.

You understand that this book is not intended as a substitute for consultation with any licensed medical, educational, or legal professional. The reader should consult with a licensed professional before making any lifestyle changes to ensure you are doing what's best for your situation and particularly with respect to any symptoms that may require diagnosis or medical attention.

Would you know my name
If I saw you in heaven?
Would it be the same
If I saw you in heaven?

I must be strong
And carry on,
'Cause I know I don't belong
Here in heaven.

Eric Clapton, Tears in Heaven

Dedicated to my dog, Max

The Grief Chronicles   1
Introduction   2
   grief is a G.I.F.T.   2

Chapter One   8
With you in my eyes like flaming flowers   8
Agony   8

Chapter Two   14
The present   14
   I am walking my dog 14

Chapter Three   17
Grief Recovery is a process   17
   And time seems eternal   17

Chapter Four   19
Something is different   19
   In the waiting room   19

Chapter Five   23
Where are you?   23
   Insanity   23

Chapter Six   31
the first of many dreams   31
   Impeccable visions of sunshine   31

Chapter Seven   34
A good day   34
   A moments relief in some stranger's arms   34

Chapter Eight   41
There are groups 41
   for grief recovery   41

Chapter Nine   44
A horrible day   44
   Sometimes well meaning friends are not useful   44

Chapter Ten   53
Therapy 53
   Have you lost interest in normal activities?   53

Chapter Eleven   56
The Real Work Begins   56
   You've got to walk that lonesome highway   56

Chapter Twelve   60

Get a grip   60
    Grief Recovery is a Process   60
Chapter Thirteen 64
Grief is a G.I.F.T. 64
    grief is a form of tender   64
Chapter Fourteen   67
Grief is a G.I.F.T. 67
    grief is for tribute   67
Chapter Fifteen   69
Grief is a G.I.F.T. 69
    Grief is for trial   69
Chapter Sixteen   72
Grief is a G.I.F.T. 72
    Grief is for Tears   72
Chapter Seventeen   76
The stopping place   76
    Now that we have rested   76
Chapter Eighteen   78
The mourning of crows.   78
    It is said that crows are very intelligent creatures.   78

ACKNOWLEDGEMENTS

Above all I would like to thank my daughter, one of the most beautiful souls I have ever known. Then I would like to thank all the thousands of families who are living this sad journey with me. This is a journey that no parent or family wants to take, but a journey that, unfortunately, many of us have had thrust upon us.

I also wish to thank my family, my daughter and son, and friends who have stood by me during some pretty fierce trials by fire.

FORWARD

This is the chronicle of my grief recovery after my daughter's death by heroin overdose at age 32 in 2009. In writing this chronicle, I initially struggled with whether or not to make this story personal to just one unique set of circumstances, the death of a loved one, in my case my beloved child, by overdose. Because of course, grief is universal. Much of what I experienced after my daughter died from an opiate overdose is applicable to all families and people suffering from the inexplicable mysteries of grief. But I also feel that when someone dies from something that has a societal stigma attached to it, as a death by heroin overdose does, that it also adds another dimension of grief for the grieving survivors. Nonetheless, there are sections of this book that others who are grieving the death of a loved one may find comforting, and I hope that they do.

My daughters name was Mary Elizabeth Mickelsen, but I will use her name sparingly for purposes of this story. Australian aborigines believe that to speak someone's name after they have died is to call them back. And I no longer wish to call her back. But in the beginning, I called her name every minute of every day.

I hope that my chronicle may help others who wander through the desolate valley of grief to find some comfort and solace. You may never fully recover from a grief so deep that it feels like it has pulverized all the bones in your body, so much that your entire foundation has collapsed, but perhaps one day you will find you have grown new bones and can walk upright again.

Introduction
grief is a G.I.F.T.
GRIEF IS A FORM OF TRANSFORMATION

Grief is a gift. Grief is the greatest form of transformation that exists for us. This is not something that you are going to want to hear in the beginning of your grief process. But grief is a necessary part of the process that opens our heart to the healing that is required to regain ourselves after the loss of our loved one. It took me six years to comprehend this process. In the beginning, the pain of losing my daughter was so raw, that I couldn't function. Losing my daughter was agony. It was visceral. It was like having a limb amputated. I had to learn to embrace the pain. I had to learn to make my peace with the pain, to love my pain, to allow the pain to transform me, to become whatever it is that I was going to become without my eldest child. I went from being "Mary's Mom," a whole person, a fully formed identity, to being an incomplete, lost patchwork of a creature. Or so the void created by her death felt like that. In those first days after she died, my mind was constantly flooded with memories of her as a child. I constantly replayed her last days in the hospital. I thought I heard her voice everywhere. I made a shrine of her clothes, I wore her shoes, I slept with her clothes over me. I could not let her go. Later, I had a necklace made with a tiny urn with some of her ashes in it. Grief is a gift, but I didn't know that yet. Grief comes from another dimension of love. It comes in waves. It racks your soul. It opens your heart and your soul and your mind to realms that you didn't know you could experience. Prior to grief you may have experienced sadness. Before grief took up residence in your house you were unhappy. But you didn't grieve. You didn't feel like rending your clothes, in the biblical sense. You didn't feel like cutting off all your hair, wearing sackcloth and ashes, staring into a mirror to see if you still had a soul. No. When grief takes up residence in your house, you will know beyond a shadow of a doubt that even though your door locks are secure, a thief has broken in, because Grief is the shadow. Now, beyond the shadow of a doubt, you are experiencing grief. Grief is the shadow, the sister of light. Grief is a gift. Grief is a period of transformation, trial and tribulation. Remember this at all times. It will get you through your darkest hours. Grief is the great transformer and equalizer. No one is immune to it. No one.

HOW TO GRIEVE

Lay on the floor and howl. Rend your clothes and scream. Alternatively get dressed in your finest clothes, speak softly, drink tea and eat chocolate. Go and climb Mt. Everest. Travel to the ends of the earth, or travel to the ends of your bedroom. Throw a party and invite all the neighbors in. Alternatively, become a hermit and never see anybody again. Curse the gods and rail at the heavens. Alternatively, curse no one and smile sweetly. As you will discover, there is no roadmap, and there is no prescribed course of action for grieving. There are rituals for mourning, but your grieving is personal. It is about you, your soul, your beloved, and no one can teach you how to grieve. There is no curriculum for grieving, but it is something that we learn. So just wake up every day and face the music. Or turn over and go back to sleep. After all, it's your grief.

"And can it be that in a world so full and busy, the loss of one weak creature makes a void in any heart, so wide and deep that nothing but the width and depth of eternity can fill it up!"

Charles Dickens

Chapter One
With you in my eyes like flaming flowers
Agony

Week one: the landscape has changed

Everything has changed. Everything looks unfamiliar. In truth, nothing has changed, but I have. Things faraway seem closer, and things that are closer seem farther. I'm not sure when the lilac bush turned burnt orange. I must be imagining this. Colors are saturated, darker. I'm seeing everything through a lens darkly, the lens of you being gone. It's stunning. It's radical discontinuity. My mind can accept the truth of your goneness, but my heart cannot. We have just arrived home from the funeral home, and in my left hand is a shopping bag. Inside the shopping bag, is neither shoes, nor a new frock, nor the new Keurig I have been dreaming about purchasing. Inside the shopping bag, this bag with the elegant, tasteful funeral house logo, is your cremains.

You were cremated. You went up in flames like a flaming flower. I chose a tasteful, elegant, urn to keep your ashes in at home. I have no mantel, nor anyplace to realistically place the urn, so to keep the urn at home is what I now call a radically discontinuous decision, like a multitude of other radically discontinuous decisions suddenly thrust upon us. Decisions: such as to plan an unwanted and unwelcome funeral for my 32-year-old daughter, who died suddenly, messily and ignobly of a heroin overdose. I say suddenly loosely, because with an addict in the family, a sudden death is always to be expected, but are we really ever prepared for death? Is it really ever easy to plan a funeral for a 32-year-old who was so full of life, hope and beauty? A young woman who just last week had gotten out of rehab, again, and promised to be clean, again, and then enrolled in college, again, and rode her bike for three miles to go register at the university registrar, on the very day that she then overdosed and died?

But this is not a story about the Heroin addict. I already wrote that story. This is a story about the numbing pain I experienced after losing my daughter. The paralyzing grief experienced after losing someone I loved so much that I thought I could never recover from this excruciating experience. People die every day. People die, but not my daughter. And not from a needle stuck in her arm, in a bathroom, behind a closed door while her junkie compatriots were less than two feet away in the same apartment. If they hadn't been junkies, shooting up themselves, they might have realized she had been gone too long behind that closed door and called 911. And, as circumstances later turned out, she possibly did not die even from her opiate of choice, Heroin. But quite possibly from a bad batch of Fentanyl, which had been making the rounds in Detroit. Fentanyl was even worse than heroin, and shooting it meant instantaneous death.

The emotional pain I experienced the bleak day she overdosed is a transcendent grief. Something that has eclipsed all former experience, and kept me frozen, paralyzed in some kind of shadow zone of perpetual grayness. As an interior designer by vocation, in describing this grey I might have told a client it was Halo Grey, or Harbor Grey, or any of the infinitely poetic grey names that paint chips have on them. But in my new reality, it was just dull grey. Cloudy, murky, ugly grey. The grey of rainy, cloudy winter skies when you wish the sun would just break through and burn off the greyness, or better yet, as I now knew, the grey of cremains in a funereal urn. I ponder a new paint color chip called "Cremains Grey".

Why write about it now? It has been six years, and in truth it has taken this long to process the emotion to the point where I can write about the experience. I use the term recover loosely, as there is no absolute, finite recovery from profound grief. Rather, there is an unfolding, like the petals of a rose opening. Little by little, step by step we learn to embrace and accept the alternate reality, the reality that we never in a million years dreamed would happen when our lovely bouncing baby was born. When planning a future for our child, we never planned for a future that included death by overdose. We never dreamt that someday this lovely bouncing baby would die of an opiate overdose with a needle stuck in her arm, from an addiction to heroin, heroin made and manufactured from beautiful red poppies that were possibly grown in the mountains of Afghanistan, manufactured into heroin, and then consequently distributed and somehow made it to Main Street USA.

The death of a child is a unique grief. It is the end not only of a life, but of all the hopes and future dreams for that life. As a parent, it is out of order. It is a death that is out of the natural order of things. In the natural order of life, parents are supposed to outlive their children. Children should not have their lives truncated, they should not be a tree that is cut down in its prime with no branches. The family tree has been truncated. All grief is difficult. I cannot compare the grief of losing a child to others, only to say that it is unique.

Chapter Two
The present

I am walking my dog

I am walking my dog on a glistening hot, sunny, palm tree lined street in Palm Springs, California. Four years ago I made a transition from Ann Arbor, Michigan to California. Up above, the sky is a brilliant shade of blue, and all around me are shocking pink Bougainville and Queen Palms. Two years ago I adopted an adorable mini-schnauzer puppy, Max. Max is currently the love of my life, and no doubt, my substitute baby. I am sometimes not sure how I got from "there" to "here". "There" being a grief-struck parent who lost her oldest child to an opiate overdose at age 32, to "Here" being an almost well-adjusted human being, walking her happy dog on a sunlit street in a beautiful town, far far away from where the tragedy took place.

Ann Arbor is where I lived for twenty-five years and raised my family. I may never have made the move out west, but my elderly father had retired to Palm Springs, and also my sister. My grown son moved to California for business, and eventually my middle daughter relocated from Hawaii where she was clerking as a Law Clerk to Los Angeles. So ultimately, in 2011, after Mary passed from opiate addiction in our home town of Ann Arbor in 2009, I made the transition to Palm Springs, first to take care of my elderly dad before he passed, and then consequently I made the decision to stay permanently in Palm Springs. This decision was not easy, as it also meant giving up my established long-term interior design practice, and a multitude of long-term friends, many of whom I still miss. But in the long run, it worked out. One of the good parts was putting some geographic distance between the locale where Mary died, so that I couldn't continue to visit our old haunts. I was fortunate to have some resources to make the move.

As I walk the sun drenched streets, happy to interact with my adorable pup, I feel almost content. If there is any truth to the timeworn adage that "time heals all," then perhaps walking your dog down a peaceful street six years after a tragedy is living proof. I sometimes feel guilty for being happy. This is called survivors guilt. I know I shouldn't be feeling this, but I do. I often question why I should be here, when my daughter who had her whole life still in front of her is gone. But I have been advised not to follow this train of thought. I am here, and that is that. The thought remains however, an ongoing, painful thought.

But my journey as to how I arrived on this street is what this saga is all about.

Chapter Three
Grief Recovery is a process

And time seems eternal
I have my good days and my bad days

At first most days are bad. In the beginning, all days are bad. Eventually, there are some not as bad days. Six years after, many days are good days, interspersed with a few bad days. This is when you may begin to believe that you have recovered from grief. That the things you have discovered about yourself, changes that you have put into motion, a certain strength and ability to survive tragedy, actually have begun to take root and work. But in the beginning, when you were raw and in pain, most days were bad. Grief comes in great waves that wash over you like the ocean at the shore. The waves recede, then come back and knock you down again. You lost your child to one of the weirdest, most horrible, incomprehensible diseases known to mankind. And many people, strangers and friends both, don't even believe addiction is a disease. Some people even believe that your child had a choice in the matter of their addiction. That this addiction was a great weakness of character. At times, you thought the same thing. You knew better, but still you had that thought, for when somebody you love is an addict, you can't help but believe the worst in them, as you watch their downward spiral. Yes, you had already been in the Bermuda Triangle of addiction with your addict for many years, the no-mans land of your loved one using an opiate. But you always thought your loved one would return from that no-mans land. Now the answer is final. They didn't make it out alive, and they're not coming back.

Chapter Four
Something is different

In the waiting room
I am in the hospital waiting room

It is a room that I am well acquainted with. Because my daughter is a long-term heroin addict, she has overdosed on more than one occasion. We have ended up in this hospital waiting room many times.

Typically, she is administered CPR, oxygen, made to drink charcoal, and she is brought back from death's door. So I am alarmed, but not as much as I should have been. Typically, a nurse always comes out to see me and tell me that Mary is fine, and that I can go back and see her. And then we start making plans to put her in yet another rehab, depending on what her insurance will pay for. But this night everything is taking longer than normal. This night something is different and I am growing very impatient. I go to the front desk to get some information, but I am told there is none. And something feels wrong. Really wrong.

And then it happens. A nurse comes out to find me, and asks me if I want to talk to the Hospital Chaplain. This has never happened before. In ten long years of fighting Mary's addiction, this has never happened. And this is when I know that something is different. That this time, she may not be returning. Hot tears fill my eyes. "I want to see my daughter" I say. "You can't see her right now" the nurse replies. "Why not?" She was brought in by ambulance and intubated. "She's critical" the nurse replies. And I am breaking down, having a hard time breathing. "Do you want to see the Chaplain?" the nurse asks again. But I am already pushing through the swinging doors to the back, determined to find my daughter. The nurse is running after me, trying to stop me, but I am determined. Fortunately, Mary is not too far back in Emergency. And there she is, on her gurney, surrounded by her medical team. Looking fresh and beautiful, except for the tube in her mouth, hooked up to a breathing machine. Still breathing. But the doctor informs me "She's only breathing because of the machine". I feel weak in the knees. Someone says "she's critical". And it really sinks in on me. My daughter is dying.

Thus began a five-day ordeal. At the end of which, we had to remove the breathing machine because she was brain dead. There was great discussion with the medical team. Was she really brain dead? Was it really irrevocable? She looked flushed and beautiful, breathing with the help of the breathing tube. But, inevitably, the truth was manifest. My beautiful daughter was gone. From a drug overdose at age 32.

There was discussion about donating her organs. After medical analysis, it was determined that her liver was in good enough shape to donate. This information was somewhat surprising, due to her concurrent alcoholism.

But, fortunately, she had also signed an organ donor release on prior visits to the hospital. So the decision was made. This turned out to be a good call, as it was somewhat gratifying when we later got a call from Gift of Life that the organ donation was complete. So in death she managed to give something that had perhaps been stolen from her during her lifetime: The Gift of Life.

Due to the nature of her death, there had to be an autopsy. This just added to the agony of planning her funeral and cremation. Her brother and sister held me up, as did other family members and friends. Everything was so grueling. The very person I wanted to talk about everything with, and lean on for support, was the one whose funeral I was planning. For despite everything, my daughter and I were the best of friends.

Chapter Five
Where are you?

Insanity
Laying on the floor clutching a photograph:
It has been eight weeks since you died. There is a deep pit in the floor of my home office. There used to be a hardwood floor in my home office, and I'm pretty sure there was no mile-deep pit to Hades. I wonder how this pit got here, this pit that must be a mile deep and goes straight to Hades. One part of me knows that I am laying prone on the hardwood floor in my home office, but another part of me feels like I am in a pit that descends to hell. Part of me suspects that I am still laying face first on the floor, but I feel like I may be in a deep pit I have just discovered somewhere in my home office that has always been here, this portal to hell that I am now sinking in, clutching a photograph of my daughter. I am sobbing deep, wracking sobs, possibly aided and abetted by too

many glasses of wine from my local pub, the pub from which I just returned, and I may be partially experiencing what is most commonly known as "being on a drunk," before I collapsed and sank into this massive emotional mastodon pit in my office floor.

I am chanting a sort of sing-song mantra, saying my daughters name over and over, "Where are you, where are you, where are you?" I can't seem to stop myself. I know that this is not healthy. I know that I should stop. I know that I should call somebody. I have had many years of therapy, and I am exquisitely practiced in the art of meditation, candle lighting, and self therapy. But right now, I am unable to stop chanting this sorrowful, ancient sounding chant of the mariners, or to light scented candles, or to calm myself. A part of me wants to stay right here in this horrendous mastodon pit, the one I have just psychically dug for myself, and wallow. This wallowing goes on interminably, maybe for an hour. Maybe two.

I live by myself. No one is here to interrupt this unmitigated sorrowful operatic chant. It is the dirge of a mother who has lost her child. It is the chant of the goddess Demeter who has lost her daughter Persephone to Hades who stole her to the underworld, and who wants her back. I am bargaining. If I bargain with the gods, they will bring my daughter back. If I am sorry enough, if I weep enough, if I do enough penance, she will come back. If I go down to the depths of the Underworld with Hades, I will be able to grab her soul and take her from the Underworld and pull her back up with me. She was not supposed to die this young. It is not the natural order of things. It is out of order. I know this. This is what this dirge is. I am singing my daughter back to me. She can hear me; I know she can. I am pitiful.

My daughter loved me. She loved me so intensely, that she used to tell me she was my Baby Whale. Mother and baby whales have an intense bond. Their bond is so intense, that if they are separated, the mother grieves for the rest of her life, and she emits, these haunting, grief struck sonar signals, signals so intense that they shatter the ocean. And the baby whale, no matter where they are in the ocean, can hear these signals. I am emitting my sonar signals. I am calling back my baby whale. My daughter is gone and I miss her with a searing, burning, visceral pain. My baby whale, my Persephone. The image of a baby whale makes me laugh out loud even through my moaning. It is this sense of humor, which I get from my father's side of the family, that helps pull me through in the long-run.

But in my heart of hearts, I know she is gone forever. Maybe she is gone because of my abysmally messed up parenting. Even though everyone keeps telling me I was a great mom. Everyone assures me that her addiction is not my fault, that she was an addict and that her choices were her own. That her death was her fault alone. That maybe her death is her drug dealers fault, the governments drug policy fault, her absentee fathers fault, but mainly her fault. But certainly not my fault. Because I did everything for her. I was the perfect mother. But in my heart of hearts, I know whose fault it is. It is my fault. I raised her. I was her example; I was her role model. Her death happened on my watch. No, I am not an addict. It doesn't matter. It is my fault and I know it. This is my sin and I will die knowing this and no one can remove the stain from me. Yes, I can be very spiritual, and even religious, and I pray all the time. But this makes matter even worse. My faith is shaken. Believe me, I know a sin when I see one. So all these idiots can tell me this is not my fault but I know better. I know. If you feel guilty for something there is a reason.

Right now, all I wish I could do is to look at her beautiful innocent angel face again and tell her that she was innocent. She had the face of an angel. I want to tell her that she was the most beautiful person in the world, and that all her own self-hatred and loathing for herself because of addiction was wrong because she was innocent. She had an addiction, and she had no choice but to use. Whereas I had a choice to be a better mother. Instead of being angry that she was using, I could have been loving. Instead of being short-tempered, I could have been patient. I could have been loving and patient. But I was not. Now I am a quivering mass of remorse and guilt.

So now I am laying on the floor, 100 feet deep in the deepest pit of Hades, clutching a photograph, her high school senior picture that she didn't even like, the photograph of herself that she hated the most, moaning and groaning and repeating like a deranged person, "Where are you?" This is an unanswerable question. Nobody knows where she is. My personal belief, because I believe in the soul, is that she is probably standing right over me with her hand on my right shoulder saying "It's OK mimetic, I love you". We are not Mexican, but she liked to call me mamacita. We both thought this was very cute. And I can hear her saying this. I can hear her laughing and saying, "Why are you laying on the floor like an idiot Mom? Get up Mom, get up. Mamacita get up." And something about hearing her voice telling me to get up suddenly snaps me out of my wallowing deranged grief and I do get up. I get on my hands and knees and realize I am indeed on the hardwood floor in my home office, not in some mile-deep mastodon pit, and I can stand up. So I stand up.

I walk to the bathroom and gaze at myself in the bathroom mirror and I look hideous. My eyes are sunken with big blue bags and my hair needs coloring and is unkempt and I look like I've aged a million years in the last two hours. In my eyes I see death and Hades and the four horsemen of the apocalypse. I hang a towel over the mirror so I don't have to look at myself anymore and go downstairs in my lovely, newly decorated townhouse. Downstairs, there are still fresh funeral flowers brought home from the funeral parlor, carefully selected and lovingly chosen from friends and family, and I make a mental note to crush them all and get rid of them in the morning.

"Crush you, my enemies" I think. I don't know if I'm referring to the dead flowers, or her drug dealers, or my sad thoughts. No wonder I'm so depressed. I'm thinking after the funeral, when all is over, people should remove all the funeral flowers. It is not cheerful and lovely for the mourner to look at all the beautifully arranged, dying funeral flowers hanging around in the living room. It's depressing. I manage to make a cup of Earl Grey tea, put on my pajamas, crawl into bed, turn off the light, and pass out.

Chapter Six
the first of many dreams

Impeccable visions of sunshine

We are sitting on a bench in my backyard

And we are thinking of baby names. The baby names we will call a little girl when you have your first child. You desperately want to be a mother. You have had a boyfriend for fifteen years, ever since you were seventeen years old. You have had one abortion because you are an addict, and everyone said you should have one and it is not fair for an addict to bring a child into the world. And yet. You regret this abortion. You desperately wanted a child. And so we are thinking of beautiful baby names because we are sure when you do have a child, that it will be a girl. In this alternate reality, you have a baby, and she is a little girl.

She is beautiful and she looks like you and she has copper hair and amber eyes. She has a creamy complexion and a radiant smile. And we are so thrilled and happy with her. We are walking on a sidewalk in California, pushing a baby stroller, because this is where we always knew we would move to, to be close to your Grandpa. We are pushing the stroller, and we can hear the ocean, and we are so happy together, and the baby, who might be named Jennifer, or Jolene, because we were stuck on J names, is burbling and happy. You are wearing that pretty white lacy gypsy boho chic hippie skirt, and the big hoop earrings that only you can carry off so well. The sound of the ocean is distant and roaring and salt spray tastes like sushi, and the sun is like a radiant impeccable vision of light and everything is shimmering and light and you are shimmering and light. You are shimmering and light because you are not real and this is only a dream, and I am dreaming, and you are not really here, and then I wake up. There is no baby girl, and you are not here, and I am still in Ann Arbor, Michigan two blocks away from where you overdosed in that apartment that your Grandpa and I rented for you. We rented it so that you would not be homeless, and at least I am eternally grateful that you did not die homeless out on the streets of Detroit or behind that infernal KFC somewhere where you always met your dealers.

Chapter Seven
A good day

A moments relief in some stranger's arms
I have my first good day.
On my first good day I manage to get out of bed and make it to the kitchen and make a fresh pot of coffee. This seems like a herculean task and after I make the coffee, I go back to bed with a fresh cup of joe and lay down again. But this was a step. The coffee, my favorite Starbucks Pikes Place, tastes dull and ashy. I seem to have lost my taste buds. I don't know if this is psychological, or if I really have lost my taste. But I figure taste maybe will come back later. The point is, I got up out of bed, and I did something normal. I probably should mention that yes, I am depressed, and yes, I have a prescription for antidepressants. They don't seem to help at all, but perhaps the motion of taking them helps, and I am taking them as the doctor prescribed.

After drinking my tasteless, ashy coffee, I decide to shower and dress. This is another momentous decision. Picking out clothes seems like just too much work, so I settle on grey sweats to match my grey mood. Chic sweats, but sweats nonetheless. I actually love beautiful clothes, so you have to understand that this is really demoralizing for me. But, again, it's a baby step. To be showered and dressed is actually a herculean task. I don't want to be showered and dressed and ready for action. I want to lay in bed all day with the blinds shut. I want to tune out the world. I can't seem to help this. I'm typically outgoing and friendly and love people. But right now I just don't want to see anybody. This is a very mixed signal to my friends. Because my friends actually want to reach out and help but I just can't seem to reciprocate. They really don't know what to do with me. Some of them just stop coming around.

But on to my good day.

I have managed to get up and get dressed and now I am sitting downstairs in my cheerful, bohemian decorated living room. I seriously don't know what to do next. Because I am self employed, I have put all my clients on the back burner. They are very understanding. Too understanding. I'm also completing a Masters Degree in Interior Design. A few years ago I made a decision to go back to university that may have been foolhardy as it is costing a fortune. But it is also giving me something to do and keeps my mind active. But today I have no studying or no real work to keep me busy. And none of my favorite pastimes are beckoning to me. Antiquing, art galleries, all smell like putrid death to me. Dead artifacts in dead spaces. No desire to go do any of that. Calling a friend to go out to lunch with someone sounds equally awful. What am I going to talk about? My dead daughter? My depressing grief? My other two adult children have flown back to their respective homes in California and Hawaii and I definitely do not want to bother them with a Sad

Mom call. I decide I need to get out in nature. Nature is restorative. So I opt for a walk in the park. This should be harmless and easy enough to accomplish at my favorite park near my house. The weather is a cool Michigan October day. I decide I am adequately dressed in my sweats. I should mention that I have been wearing my daughters old black Sketchers running shoes. They're worn out and tacky, but we wore the same size seven shoe. For some reason, I just started wearing them after she died. Looking down at my feet in her shoes feels somehow comforting.

So off I dutifully trudge to the Park. This may have not been such a great idea. In the park, there are happy shiny people, runners and mothers with babies in strollers. This, of course, makes me remember being a young mother and happier days when I had my daughter in her baby stroller. Tears begin streaming down my face. Tears are rolling down my face and they are salt tears and they are rolling out to the ocean and becoming one with the ocean and soon the Atlantic Ocean is roiling inside of me, and I am roiling and rocking like a boat adrift out at sea. I have never felt lonelier or more lost, and my walk in the park isn't going very well, so I turn back home. Suddenly a nondescript looking stranger, a larger, older woman, with gray hair, notices that I am crying. She approaches me, and I am skittish about strangers approaching me. But she says, "Dear, can I help you?" I have a paranoid thought, as if she is some kind of secret operative, like in Bourne Identity, but really she is just a kind old lady, and her kindness overwhelms me, and I manage to reply "No, I'm fine". Which is a total lie but I do not want to have a complete breakdown in front of a total stranger. But somehow she sits me down on a park bench, puts her arms around me, and I weep, right there, in the arms of a stranger. She is so kind, and she doesn't even ask me to talk. And I look up at her, and I blurt out, "My daughter just died". I feel mortified that I have just told a stranger something personal. But this kind person just says "That is so painful". And that is the kindest thing anyone has said to me so far, friend or family. After awhile, I stop crying, and she stops holding me. She gives me a tissue and we sit for awhile on the bench, and then she says, matter of factly, "It will get better Dear". And she leaves. Just like that. I begin to wonder if she was an angel, or an alien messenger, or just some very wise and kind soul. She may have been a homeless woman, or she may have been a very wealthy retiree taking a walk in the park. For once in my life, I honestly didn't even notice how she was dressed. She was just so kind. Because I feel better after she leaves. I walk home, and I feel lighter. And this is my first good day. Mind you, not a great day, but a better day. A day when I showered, dressed, left the house, and had some human communication with a total stranger, who just happened to be there, and happened to respond to a stranger who was crying. And this is how grief recovery begins. A day when you managed to get dressed, leave the house, and you, who consider yourself a rock, and who is slightly germaphobic, and ten weeks ago would have rather dropped dead than let a total stranger put their arms around you to comfort you on a public park bench, found a moment of relief in some kind strangers arms.

Chapter Eight
There are groups
for grief recovery

I do not want to join a grief group. But my father's girlfriend from California gives me the name of someone in California who has just started a grief recovery group for people whose children have died from a drug overdose. I decide to call this person. As it turns out, we have a lot in common, and we end up talking on the phone for hours and decide we are kindred spirits.

LEARNING TO COPE WITH DISENFRANCHISED GRIEF

I discover that death by opiate overdose is a national epidemic, that thousands upon thousands of young adults are dying from this epidemic, and that I am just one of many grieving parents. I also discover that my grief is called "disenfranchised" grief. In otherwords, there is a stigma attached to this type of death. It is not a socially acceptable death, say like death from a disease like cancer. So this makes talking about the way your child died in polite society even more difficult. So when people ask, "How did your daughter die", I mostly feel like lying. Sometimes I make up stories. I say she died from cancer, or in a car accident. This just compounds the agony and the grief. It is hard to feel like you have to come out of the closet about something so personal and agonizing as a death in the family, in particular the death of a child. But this is the case with death by overdose.

So compounding the grief I am experiencing for my daughter, is the fact that the way she died is disenfranchised grief, and many people misunderstand and just don't know what to say. If you said she died from cancer, or in a car accident, they would be very sympathetic. But it is much harder to say she was a heroin addict and died from a drug overdose. Many people think it was her fault, she brought it on herself, etc. Others feel it shouldn't be discussed. Some believe I was an enabler. This is a terrible thing to have heaped on the head of a parent who is experiencing grief.

This particular Grief Recovery group deals with all these issues and more and is an outlet for people who are experiencing this so-called disenfranchised grief to find sympathy with others to share their stories with. I am not much of a group joiner, but for my first two years talking to other members of the group really helps me. Eventually, as I got deeper into my recovery, I found I no longer wanted this form of expression. But in the beginning it was a huge help, and I surely recommend this form of expression for those who are struggling.

Chapter Nine
A horrible day

Sometimes well meaning friends are not useful

How did I get here?

Here being in the basement of my condo with a piece of electric cord in my hand, contemplating throwing the cord over a heating duct to end it all. The day started out normally enough, with coffee, shower, reading the paper, going for a walk, talking on the phone with friends. I felt half way human. I got some work done, even went to the gym. Cleaned the house. Life goes on. And then a well meaning friend called in the afternoon, and asked if she could stop by for awhile. "Sounds great!" I said. After all, having company over and entertaining is normal, right?

My friend is an artist, a photographer. Many of my friends are artists and musicians. She arrives with a book in hand, which inwardly makes me groan. I have the distinct feeling that she is here to "cheer me up". But I greet her warmly, as I really do appreciate the effort, and the attempt at camaraderie. I break out a bottle of the "good wine," a nice Australian Sauvignon I have been saving for quite awhile for exactly an occasion like this. An occasion when a dear friend might come over to spend some quiet, friendly time. But there is an elephant in the room. More like the Mastodon. Because no longer can I just discuss the latest gossip, culture, art, politics and current events. Everyone wants to know, "How I am doing?".

And I am not doing well. I am not doing well at all. But I can't really put this into words. I can't answer in a casual conversation. That I feel like shit most days. That all I can think of is my daughter, every minute of every day. That I don't feel like being cheerful and putting on a game face. That the Lord, whom I believe in dearly, suddenly seems to have abandoned me and is not my Rock and my Redeemer. That I am unhappy. That, to paraphrase Mick

Jagger, I "see a Red Door and I want it painted Black". That every where I go, I look for my daughter. That her face haunts me. And that worst of all, in this fast moving world, everyone thinks I should be moving on.

Yes, that's right. My mom died when I was a teenager. My Dad handled his grief with great grace and dignity. He continued on with the most amazing grace and was a solid rock in taking care of his responsibilities and family. But here am I. Still a total basket case eight months later. Maybe because it is my child. But the point is, I cannot move on very well. As a matter of fact, I cannot move on hardly at all. So when people ask me, "How are you doing?" I mostly put a frozen smile on my face and reply "Fine". But that is the absolute farthest thing from the truth you could ever get.

At any rate, my friend suspects I am lying. And she is a dearheart and very well meaning, so she is on a mission to cheer me up. And I do love her dearly. So she pulls out this book, and says, "I thought you might like to hear some readings from this book". I have actually come to hate self-help books. I've read many, and they all basically preach the same thing. Basically, they say, "You are not good enough, so read this book". I don't buy it. I know that I am good enough, and that I am just temporarily depressed. Who wouldn't be depressed after their daughter died? I just lost my child. This is depressing as hell.

But because I am polite, and well bred, I let my friend read to me. Her voice is soothing enough, and in tandem with the nice Australian Sauvignon Blanc, I start to feel a little bit mellow. Maybe this isn't so bad. The reading is exactly what I expect it to be. Somewhat bland, not too inspiring, telling me to have faith, believe in myself, believe in better days, positive affirmations, blah blah blah. And then something she says makes me sit up and take umbrage. NO. I think. NOT THIS. It is something about "Anytime you don't like something in someone else, it is a mirror.

Say it about yourself". UGH. I don't like this one bit. She says something about "If you think someone is an addict, it is really you who is the addict". Now I am visibly upset, at least to myself. What is this nonsense? Are you telling me that I, who didn't do drugs, was the addict all along? I had the addictive behavior? So I drink a little wine. So I go to the pub. So I come from a drinking family. So I may be a little bit obsessive. Now I am internally shaking. Are you saying my daughter learned addictive behaviors from me? If so, why aren't my other two adult children addicts? In the meantime, my friend has been reading along, covering some other sections. But I am stuck on this one. I can't get past it. It's really traumatizing me.

The evening wears on, and after awhile I feign that I am tired, and my friend acquiesces and leaves. And I am very internally traumatized. Furious. Guilt and pain are consuming me. This was the worst session with a friend ever. Not only am I not comforted, I am despondent. I want to off myself. This would be terribly selfish, but I am not in my right mind and I don't care. I'm not thinking straight, about my other children, or how this would affect anyone else. I'm thinking about how I will end this psychic pain, and be with my daughter.

I am not typically suicidal, but I have a horrible feeling in my gut. Suddenly I despise myself. I have gone downstairs to get the laundry, so now I am in the basement, which is quasi-finished, and has all these ugly overhead heating ducts, that as a designer I painted white hoping to mitigate how ugly they are, hoping they would look post-industrial chic. Now they just look post industrial chic perfect for a potential suicide. I see some electrical wire sitting on a chair. I grab the wire, and contemplate wrapping it round my neck, then standing on a nice sturdy craftsman style chair, which also suddenly looks perfect for a potential suicide, and tying one end of the wire around the post industrial painted white heating duct. I even wrap the wire around my neck. And then, I swear, I hear my daughters voice saying "Mamacita! What are you doing? Mamacita, don't be a silly goose!?" And I snap out of this extreme suicidal despondency and idiocy. I think I would not have really followed through, but this is the closest I have ever come to even thinking such thoughts. Did I really hear her voice? I did. Was it really her? I can't say. But I put down the electrical cord, forget about the laundry like I have seen a ghost, and scurry as fast as I can upstairs to my lovely romantic turquoise and white bedroom, which suddenly, after the post-industrial chic hell in the basement, and the mastodon pit in my home office, feels like I just surfaced into shabby chic mecca, and lay down in my extremely soft, comforting bed. I am not an atheist. I pick up an old bedside Bible for comfort and read a favorite passage. "But they that wait upon the Lord shall renew their strength; they shall mount up with wings as eagles; they shall run, and not be weary; and they shall walk, and not faint." Oddly, I had found this passage written in my daughter's journals also.

Peace.

Something shifts back to normal and I am feeling comforted. I am still irrationally furious with my friend and swear not to let anyone in the house for awhile. I fall into a fitful sleep. In the morning, I am duly appalled at last nights' behavior. What a horrible night. And I also realize what a razor sharp tightropes edge I have really been walking on since you died. I now know for an indisputable fact not that I am not all right. I realize I need something more than just the distant grief group in California, and talking to my friend. My friend is a certified Grief Counselor, but she is also swamped with hundreds of people calling her daily because she is the head of her burgeoning overdose organization. I decide to start some serious counseling with a local grief therapist.

Chapter Ten
Therapy

Have you lost interest in normal activities?
This seems like a trick question.

Basically, I have lost interest in everything. Especially music. Music, which used to be my life, my refuge, and my greatest joy, is now my greatest pain. I can't stand to listen to any kind of music anymore. Especially, soft soothing music. Everything makes me cry now. Rock, classical, and especially soothing music. Every single song reminds me of my loss and brings tears to my eyes. There is no safe song. Sesame street songs. Ernie singing is the worst. Rolling Stones songs. Classical. Beethoven. It doesn't matter. They all make me cry. I'm a pianist and playing my piano makes me cry. So basically, I have shut down all music. Since we live in a musical society, where everything has music or Muzak, this is difficult. Even being on hold on the phone to Time Warner Cable has Musak which can make me cry. Music triggers memories, and memories make me cry.

The therapist decides we should up my anti-depressants. And have me see a shrink. This sounds even more depressing to me, since I am very independent. I think it is ironic that the answer to my grief and issues is more drugs. I'm not sure this is what I need, but I promise I'll think about it. In the meantime, I continue talking on the phone to the head of the grief recovery organization, my grief person in California who also lost her son to opiate overdose. This person is also a certified Grief counselor. She is wonderful. She is much more helpful than my local therapist, as she has actually experienced the loss of a child from heroin overdose. She is so helpful. But really, I am grasping at straws. Deep down I know: the only answer is inside myself. I must dig deep inside myself for strength. I must examine all of my beliefs. I must find the reason to go on with life and living myself. I must find my own answers, my own beliefs, and my own reasons for living. This is the only way.

So begins my own Grief Journey.

Chapter Eleven
The Real Work Begins

You've got to walk that lonesome highway
You've got to walk it by yourself with your mental grief trucking boots

I have the lyrics to some old song stuck in my head.

Because it's the truth. I am on some highway, and it is long and it is lonely, and no one else can walk it for me. I must go on and find the route that will save me from despair and loneliness and grief. There are few markers, though many have traveled. But so many families and parents are on this particular grief highway right now, its like an army.

It is a highway and overhead is a big sign that says "People who loved someone who died from opiate overdose". And on this highway is an army of families and loved ones who have lost loved ones to opiate or heroin overdose, and who are marching in lockstep together in grief. So maybe I need to lead the charge. Because I am also a poet and a writer and goddammit, I am my father's daughter and I am part stoic and I can do this. You've got to walk that lonesome highway. And I think I hear my daughters voice saying "Come on mamacita, get trucking".

So I put on my mental grief trucking boots. I begin by pulling out my home library of sacred books. Besides for being a designer, I'm also an erstwhile bookworm and poet and philosopher. I have a library shelf of books that are just for my philosophical and sacred books, books that encompass everything philosophical and spiritual: Zen Buddhism, Torah, Bible, Tao Te Ching, I Ching, yes, Fairy Wicca, Socrates, Aristotle, and Carl Jung. I figure this is as good a place to start as any to find some wisdom beyond my tortured little mind. I also pull out my favorite poets: Rilke, Browning, Yeats, Auden, the ever gloomy Emily Dickinson, and e.e. Cummings. Poetry of course is also a window into wisdom. The Wisdom of the Ages. I am immersed in the wisdom of the ages. So now, I am sitting on my floor at home, in Lulumon active clothes, with the wisdom of the ages around me, and a cup of Jasmine tea. This feels good, like perhaps I am on the right track. I'm not really sure, but maybe. I have a pen in my hand so I can underline whatever sage comments I see.

Two hours later I am emotionally and mentally exhausted. Perhaps this was overly ambitious. Too much wisdom of the ages for one session. Maybe I need the Cliff notes? I feel somewhat drained, no wiser. But I am fortunate. Because my daughter was a poet and a writer, and she left a journal of poetry and notes and her favorite writings. And in these journals, I can find the sensitive soul that she was. And also some of the quotes that sustained her through her darkest hours.

So I pull out her notebooks and journals. All handwritten in cursive. She also spent quite a bit of time in jail on petty theft and drug charges, so she had plenty of time to read and write. And write she did. After she died, her brother and sister made copies and compiled everything into notebooks. For the most part, I haven't been able to bear looking at her journal entries and poetry. But suddenly I realize I need to take a look.

It's both sobering and chilling look into her soul and her memories. I find a sensitive and tormented soul that yearned to be free of her addiction. I knew she was tormented, but reading her writings and journal makes me break down again. Such hope, despair, and beauty. Faith and misery all combined into one gorgeous, wrenching story. A story that I've come to realize is very familiar to those who lose loved ones to addiction. Typically, addicts are beautiful, sensitive, creative, incredibly wonderful souls. Filled with love and yearning, and undying hope and belief that one day they will be clean and normal. Until the day they overdose.

Chapter Twelve
Get a grip

Grief Recovery is a Process
Get a GRIP

is my new mantra... It has come after much trial and error. Two steps forward, four steps backwards. Nights of leaving the warmth of my secure condo and walking over the two blocks to the apartment complex where my daughter overdosed. At the complex I stand at the foot of the steps where the ambulance came and picked her up and spirited her away to the hospital. If I hear someone coming, I nonchalantly walk on, as if I am out and about for an evening stroll. But I'm not. I'm trying to conjure up my daughter. To relive her last moments. One of her old junkie cohorts still lives in this complex. I detest this girl. I think it may have been this girl who gave her the bad junk, but I have no proof. It really doesn't matter now.

I know how unhealthy my behaviors are becoming. I am aware that I am becoming lost and pathetic. I still have a life outside of my daughter's death. I have friends, work, and even school. Before she passed, I had returned to University to complete a long abandoned college Degree. The studies have actually helped to keep me sane. So it's not that I don't have anything to occupy myself with.

In the interim I also take a trip to Hawaii to see my other adult daughter. The trip is refreshing and poignant. We cry together, and we spread some of Mary's ashes in Hawaii. Later, her sister takes some of her ashes to Machu Picchu and spread some ashes there. So my daughter had quite the sending off. And yet. I still return to the place where she overdosed. I am haunted.

I have been contemplating moving to California. This is not a sudden decision; I have been thinking about it for many years. My father and sister live there. And my son has relocated to San Diego. And I am getting closer to retirement age. I love Ann Arbor but I am so haunted here. It is hard to walk down the streets where she walked, to breathe the air she breathed, to go downtown to the restaurants we used to frequent. It all makes me crazy. I need to get a grip.

I have exhausted my mental, spiritual and emotional resources. The late night phone calls to friends. The counseling with the grief group. The spiritual books I read. I was raised a secular Jew. I love Judaism. I am neither atheist nor agnostic. I love the ancient prayers. The Lord is my Rock and my Redeemer. Blessed is Israel. I lift up my eyes to the mountains from whence cometh my strength. I believe this with all my heart and soul and mind. But I am still despondent. My faith is shaken. I can't help it. I'm not angry. I'm not bitter. I just can't find the will to go on. I am shaken to the core of my being. My daughter is gone. A part of me has died. People die every day. Other people lose children. Some in more horrible ways. This doesn't matter to me. All I know now is that I am raw. I feel like an idiot for feeling like this. My family seems stoic to me. What is wrong with me? Grief Recovery is a Process. I need to get a grip.

I begin recording some meditations.

Chapter Thirteen
Grief is a G.I.F.T.

grief is a form of tender

Tender is how we pay for something, as in the legal tender. Tender is also a feeling, as in we feel tender about someone or something, a feeling of tenderness. Grief is a form of emotional tenderness; it is the tender with which we pay our last emotional respects to someone who has died. It is our emotional payment to our beloved; our tender to their life for everything they did for us and for everything we felt for them. The more we loved someone, the more tender we will feel after their passing, that is, the more emotional tender we will wish to pay them.

Some debts can never be repaid. The largest debt of all is the emotional debt we owe to our beloved child. As a child, they gave us unconditional love. Perhaps later, as the adult addict, that love was compromised. Perhaps as the adult addict, they did horrible, what may have seemed at the time like unforgivable acts. Perhaps they stole from us, or abused us when they were in the throes of their addiction. They may have said horrible things. We in turn may have responded with equally bad, terrible emotional responses.

So now, in our grief, we pay our emotional tender. Grief is a gift. It is the payment that makes everything even. It is the payment of our emotional karma, the evening of the scales, the payment of our soul to make things right. It opens up the portals to forgiveness, forgiveness of ourselves and of our loved one. As we grieve, all is cleared away. We are purified. We know in our heart of hearts that we loved our child with all of our heart. If we could have them back for just one moment, we would hold them and never let them go. We would tell them that all is forgiven. It is our grief that has opened our eyes and our hearts and our minds. Our tender helps us to heal and come back to our senses. We can't see in the beginning that grief is a gift.

But in the end it is a gift that will help us to heal. We will pay our tender. And in the paying, the scales will be more balanced, and we will become more whole.

Chapter Fourteen
Grief is a G.I.F.T.

grief is for tribute

Grief is the tribute we give to the life that our loved one has lived. Because they lived their life, we pay tribute to their time on this earth. It seems odd that one would celebrate a life with grief, but in the beginning, this is the initiation that all souls perform. Our grief is the very instrument that is the most meaningful tribute on earth. If someone dies and you are indifferent to their death, then they are a stranger to your heart and house. They have no meaning to you at all.

It is the grief you feel at a passing that is the fitting tribute to a life well lived. Yes, celebrations may come later, wakes and meals and remembering the good times. But in the first hours and days, it is the bone-crushing grief that is really the fitting tribute to your loved one. Grief is the house built of gold and diamond, the cathedral inside your mind that goes up to the sky with spires and parapets, and that is built with the mortar of the aching love in your heart and soul, and whose roof is cemented with your tears. This cathedral of grief is the tribute that no King can force his subjects to build; it is the tribute that every person who loves someone builds by themselves, psychic brick by brick. Grief is a g.i.f.t: grief is the fitting tribute to the depth of the love you carry in your heart for your loved one. The memorial you have built inside your mind, this cathedral of grief, is the fitting tribute to the life of your loved one, built on the shared memories of every moment of the life you shared together.

Chapter Fifteen
Grief is a G.I.F.T.

Grief is for trial

Grief is the trial we go through after a loved one has passed. A trial can have a twofold meaning. A trial can be something we pass through, such as a trial by fire. Or a trial can be a jurisprudence, such as when someone breaks the law, and must be judged by a jury of their peers and a judge. Either way, a trial is something that must be endured, and wherein we are judged. In the case of grief, we are judging how well we behaved towards our love one. We are judging every moment and second we spent with them. We are reviewing our entire history with our loved one, the good moments and the bad moments. We want to cherish the good moments, and we are judging the bad moments. Grief is our trial by fire, our trial of ourselves as to how we behaved. Perhaps we wish we could take back the words we said that we didn't mean. Perhaps we wish we could go back and undo some of the things that we did. Or perhaps we wish we would have spent more time with our loved one. Perhaps we wish for the missed opportunities to have been with them. We are going through a period of trial for ourselves. Sometimes grief is the harshest trial of all, wherein we are acting as judge and jury on ourselves. It is best during the period of grief to try and forgive ourselves for our own past errors. To try to love ourselves as we know that our loved one loved us. For they themselves would not have put us on trial. Grief is a gift. Grief is for trial. Grief is for a trial of our strength as a human being, for a trial of our faith in whatever God we believe in, a trial of our willingness to go on living and accept that we must accept life on its own terms. Grief is for a trial of our willingness to open our hearts to other people, the living people who remain in our lives, who need us and who are with us still, and not shut out the beautiful world that continues to exist around us. Grief is the greatest trial we may ever go through as a soul, but we must accept that in the end, we have no choice, but to accept grief as a gift. For in this acceptance, the trial will be adjudicated and we will begin to move on. At some point, we have to end the trial, accept the consequences, stop judging ourselves. Nobody remains in court forever. At some point, the jury declares the verdict. The sentence is pronounced. Our loved one is gone. Now the time for judgment is past. The trial has been ended, the jurors have gone home. Grief is a gift, and the sooner we accept the verdict, the sooner we will be free to move on.

Chapter Sixteen
Grief is a G.I.F.T.

Grief is for Tears

You have shed more tears than you thought you were capable of crying. You have shed so many tears that you have watered the garden of Eden, and lilies and roses are growing in your bedroom, from your bedroom coverlet and everywhere you turn, out of your bathtub and shower, and spreading tendrils into your living room. You cannot turn off the spigot, your tears fall at the slightest memory of your child. You cannot help yourself from looking at baby pictures, and even if you were to throw out all the albums, the pictures are still in your mind, etched like fine daguerreotypes. Every single memory from the time your child came out of the womb, to the time they took their first step, to their first day at school, is haunting you, and every single memory brings forth a new crystalline teardrop. Your eyes keep watering and you can't keep enough tissues and handkerchiefs. Your eyes have turned blue from crying. Your eyes are puffy and blue and you look like you have been beat up because you have been beat up. You have been beat up by tears.

A tear is also a rip, something that tears fabric asunder. A tear has been made in the fabric of your world. It will take time to mend this tear. Tears are cleansing and tears are purifying and tears are awful, or full of awe. They roll down your face and onto your clothes and they are part of the river of life. Tears water the gardens in your mind, the gardens of your memories. And these gardens need to be watered. They need to be watered so they can flourish and grow. For in these gardens are the memories of everything good that is a part of you. Your child is part of your flesh, bone of your bone and blood of your blood. There was a silver, invisible cord that tied you together since birth. An invisible cord tied you together so that you always knew where your child was and if your child was hurting, and when your child was happy. And that cord has been cut. But maybe it hasn't. Maybe it still exists, somewhere out in the ether. You really can't be sure. You don't really want to be sure.

In the Jewish tradition, we sit Shiva. This is a seven-day mourning period, wherein it is believed that the soul is still taking leave of the body. It is a period of saying goodbye to the soul. It is mostly a time for the mourner to say goodbye and to prepare to re-enter the outside world after this period of mourning. The mourning does not end, but this specific period is very helpful. Other traditions have other similar periods of respect and respite. I personally feel these traditions are valuable and have been handed down through generations for many reasons. I feel each individual should do and follow whatever they feel is right for them. But personally, I feel that our culture is so unprepared for death and the mourning process. A time for reflection and a step back from worldly concerns to me is a good thing. It may not be possible due to work and other family concerns. But I wish there was more credence and time given for the tears to flow freely and the magnitude of the loss to be experienced.

And what if you find you can't cry? That your eyes are dry as the Sahara Desert? This is fine too. Maybe you are a person with the opposite reaction. Maybe your tears are internal. Maybe the "tear" is an internal rending. You are feeling the pain but your physical eyes are dry. Grief is a gift and grief is for tears. Tears are made in the fabric of life. Your life has been torn asunder nonetheless. Cry in your own fashion, with the silent cries of your heart. Your own heart will hear you and your silent tears will water the garden of your memories and soul just as surely as your more water prone compatriots. Grief is for tears. Grief is a gift.

Chapter Seventeen
The stopping place
Now that we have rested

We must move forward. There is no other way to go. Grief has been our stopping place. It has been, in reality, the place we have stopped. We didn't feel like we were resting, but we were. We were resting in a cocoon where we were sheltered from the rest of the world. Friends, family, and maybe life itself sheltered us while we had time to grieve. We didn't pay attention to the many good things surrounding us, hopefully a roof over our heads, food on the table, places to go mourn. We have been locked inside our self like a turtle withdrawn into the house on its back. But in a sense, we have indeed rested. We have stopped the world. But now that we have stopped, slowly, inexorably and surely, we are starting to move on with our little baby turtle tracks.

So it from this stopping place that I would like to offer a summary of some of my more pertinent strategies that helped me advance in my stages of grief. Not a program, but my simple summary. Please don't groan inwardly. Everyone moves at their own pace. What helped me may not help you. There is no set timetable for grief recovery. It is an ongoing process. But I hope that my journey might bring some comfort to others. Yes, it does get better.

Chapter Eighteen
The mourning of crows.

It is said that crows are very intelligent creatures.

It is said that crows, who mate for life, recognize when one of their kind has died. And that they bring sticks, and stones and place these sticks and stones on the body of their fallen comrades. And other crows gather round. As such, they have a type of funeral for a fallen crow. If even a bird can have a funeral, and mourn for a fallen bird, and have some type of ritualistic funerals, then how much more so should we, as human beings, have our own rituals, our own mourning period, our own grieving period?

ALLOW YOURSELF TIME TO MOURN.

In our rushed and time-pressured society, we have few mourning rituals. The time-honored rituals of your own childhood religion are there for a reason. Follow them, or follow your own. I believe that mourning is universal, it is innate, and needs to be honored. A period of mourning is different from grief. Mourning is a process of mourning the departure of the beloved. It is saying good-bye to the physical body and soul. This is the period of funeral, of ritual, of service. Mourning is followed by grieving. Grieving is then the process of learning how to live without them. This period is indeterminate. Understand that this is a necessary rite of passage. I believe we are born knowing how to mourn; this is innate. But grieving is a process we learn, we come to understand, and eventually we come to recognize. Oh yes, this is what we are doing, we are grieving.

TRAGEDY BY ITS VERY DEFINITION DOES NOT MAKE SENSE

SO DO WHAT MAKES SENSE FOR YOU.

Do not allow yourself to be pressured by others expectations for you. Your grief is yours and yours alone.

There is not a set timetable for anything concerning your grief recovery, your rituals, or your beliefs. Your grief belongs to you, and you alone. Own it.

NO MAN IS AN ISLAND, UNLESS THEY WANT TO BE

REACH OUT TO FRIENDS, FAMILY, AND COMMUNITY As you can, when you can. Allow friends and family to reach out to you. As you can, when you can. Sometimes you will want to see people, and sometimes you will not. Sometimes you will want to slam the door in peoples face. Your true friends will not be angry with you. They will love you no matter what. Respect your own boundaries.

SHOWING EMOTION IS NOT A SIGN OF WEAKNESS

BE AWARE THAT YOU ARE FRAGILE. Be aware that you are in a fragile emotional state. In the age of Iron Man and Iron Woman, it is sometimes taken as a sign of weakness to display emotion. Sometimes taking antidepressants is seen as "using a crutch". This is not a crutch; it is a sign of strength that you want to take good care of yourself. Eat and exercise the best you can. For me, Nature is restorative. Take walks as you can. But if all you can do is take a walk to the Living Room at first, congratulate yourself on baby steps.

PERHAPS GET A PET

If you don't already have a faithful companion, whether human, canine or feline, and if you are able, consider getting a pet. The love and companionship of my dog has personally helped me tremendously. At least for me, it's hard to stay sad when confronted with a happy doggy face. But it was four years after before I got Max.

HELPING OTHERS IS THE BEST ANTIDOTE TO BEING STUCK IN YOUR OWN PROBLEMS AND WORRIES

CONTINUE ON WITH AS MANY LIFE ACTIVITIES AS POSSIBLE Easier said than done, I know. But the more you can continue on with your job, your hobbies, your studies, and your life in the community, the more at ease you might begin to feel. Someday that frozen smile plastered on your face may actually begin to turn into a real smile. You may even begin to laugh again.

SEEK FRIENDS WHO DO NOT JUDGE YOU

This seems like a no-brainer, but it can be difficult if old friends seem to have any judgment on you, or if new people you meet get that funny look on their face when you tell them your child or loved one died of an opiate overdose. Avoid these people like the plague. You don't need them. And you may find that you find fellowship with new friends.

I also became very active on social media. It helps that I am a creative. Through my Instagram account, I found a like-minded community of photographers, artists, and poets, whose encouragement helped me to write this book, and develop my artistry. This quiet community of global friends helped fill a void, as it is always there, 24/7.

I formed a new personal mission to help uplift and inspire others through the only tools I have, my creativity and art.

SEEK COUNSELING IF NECESSARY

Seek counseling if you feel like you need it. Interact with grief groups, or other groups who lend you support. Speak with your ministers or Rabbis. If you prefer to fly solo, there are still a lot of on-line resources where you can at least touch base with knowledgeable people in a more anonymous fashion, and with others who can help fill in the gaps in your darkest hours. For awhile I took to dialing phone psychics. Yes, judge me if you will. But some of them turned out to be very compassionate, a voice to listen to me, and got me through some very dark moments. I say, "Whatever gets you through the moment".

THE EMPTY CHAIR AT THE TABLE

Prep yourself for the holidays. Holidays are the worst. They really are. So you must take serious steps in preparation. I find I am never more depressed than when the holidays are approaching. Of course, I have other adult children to celebrate with. And, oh yeah, THAT.

Sometimes people will say to me, "Well, at least you have two OTHER children". As if somehow that makes losing my oldest daughter any less painful. And I always have to struggle when people ask me "How many children do you have?" (Three.) But back to the holidays. The best way to deal is to basically just realize that, holidays are going to be difficult. They are going to suck. Someone is going to be missing. There is always going to be an empty chair at the table. So as the "holidays" approach, I always just try and mentally prepare myself as best I can. For me, I look at pictures of my daughter. I tell her I miss her. I tell her I wish she was here, celebrating with us. And then I try to enjoy everyone else as best I can. And I try to focus on the present time, and reflect on how lucky I am that I had my daughter with me for the sacred time that she was here with me. For she was the daughter of life, and did not just belong to me. She belonged to life itself.

BE TOUGH IN YOUR OWN LITTLE WAY.

Yes, I know I just told you to be emotionally vulnerable, and now I am telling you to be tough. So contradictory. I do apologize. But you do have to be a little bit tough. So perhaps you thought this was going to be a tale of how I traveled to some exotic land, how I left everything behind, and how I met fellow travelers on some road to Zanzibar to recover from my grief. Perhaps you thought this was going to be a story of redemption, of how I lost myself in booze and then found myself on some street corner or dark alley, and then got my life back together again. No, rather this is the story of how I went deep inside myself and found a reservoir of strength in my day to day existence, in the small motions and rituals of ordinary life. For many of us do not have the luxury of "leaving it all behind". We must move forward, inch by inch, increment by increment, waking up each day to face a world that seems so empty to us now, climbing an internal mountain every single day, an epic mountain taller than Mt. Everest, a mountain that the outside world cannot view. So to you, fellow grief travelers, I say, be tough in your own little way. Put on your little grief knapsack with all the little grief supplies in it, ropes and pulleys, and trudge your way up the grief mountain. Because I'll be waiting for you at the top.

AND MOST OF ALL.

LOOK INWARD TO FIND YOUR STRENGTH. You have within you a deep reservoir of strength. It is deeper than you can imagine. It is the strength of a mother that nurtured her children and stayed up with a sick child all night, the strength of a person that carried the weight of supporting a family. It is the strength of the mountains that do not crumble to the seas, it is the strength of your loved one's love that is assuredly reaching through the firmament and wants you to go on and live life. For love is a whole ingredient, and it can never be broken or diminished, not even by death. Your strength is inside of you and it is nurtured by the love you carry for your beloved. Cherish their memories and all the good times, the times that you had with them on this earth. Do not begrudge them the happy memories, for this would be to deny the very meaning of their time on earth. Look inward to find your strength, and you will be carried along by all the other people who travel with you, the ones who have come before you, the ones who have yet to come, the ones who are with you at all times, saying, "Keep on moving, keep on moving, keep on moving".

Marie Minnich
Mother of Mary Elizabeth Mickelsen

March 2016

ADDENDUM-POEMS

When Will I Be Myself Again
by Rabbi Lewis John Eron

"When will I be myself again?"
Some Tuesday, perhaps,
In the late afternoon,
Sitting quietly with a cup of tea,
And a cookie;
Or Wednesday, same time or later,
You will stir from a nap and see her;
You will pick up the phone to call her;
You will hear her voice – unexpected advice –
And maybe argue.
And you will not be frightened,
And you will not be sad,
And you will not be alone,
Not alone at all,
And your tears will warm you.
But not today,
And not tomorrow,
And not tomorrow's tomorrow,
But some day,
Some Tuesday, late in the afternoon,
Sitting quietly with a cup of tea,
And a cookie;
And you will be yourself again.

Do Not Stand At My Grave And Weep
by Mary Elizabeth Frye

Do not stand at my grave and weep I am not there.
I do not sleep.
I am a thousand winds that blow.
I am the diamond glints on snow.
I am the sunlight on ripened grain.
I am the gentle autumn rain.
When you awaken in the morning's hush I am the swift uplifting rush Of quiet birds in circled flight.
I am the soft stars that shine at night.
Do not stand at my grave and cry; I am not there.
I did not die.

Authors Note:

There are many grief recovery organizations available to help you through your turmoil. I do not endorse any particular one, for many are good. Just do an internet search on "Grief Recovery" or "Grief Recovery Overdose" and you will find a wealth of helpful resources. Find the one that resonates with you and your beliefs.

AUTHOR BIO

Marie Minnich currently lives in Palm Springs, California with her pooch, Max. She splits her time between her writing, photography, her interior design business, playing her piano, social media, and walking her dog. Besides being an advocate of changes in drug policy, she is also a huge advocate for rescue dogs.

Made in the USA
Las Vegas, NV
16 June 2025